THE
VICTORIAN KITCHEN
Book of
CAKES & COOKIES

THE
VICTORIAN KITCHEN
Book of
CAKES & COOKIES

ISLAND BOOKS
PRODUCED FOR S. WEBB & SON

The Victorian Kitchen Book Collection

Designed, written and edited by
THE BRIDGEWATER BOOK COMPANY LTD

Text Amelia Swann
Art Director Annie Moss
Designer Jane Lanaway
Managing Editor Anna Clarkson
Page make-up Chris Lanaway
Photographer Trevor Wood
Hand-coloured plates Lorraine Harrison
Food preparation and styling Jon Higgins

Every effort has been made to trace all copyright
holders. The publishers sincerely apologise for
any inadvertant omissions and will be happy to
correct them in any future edition.

CLB 4187

This edition published by S. Webb & Son

© 1995 CLB Publishing
Godalming, Surrey

Colour separation by Sussex Repro, England
Printed and bound in Singapore

ISBN 1-85833-459-4

CONTENTS

INTRODUCTION

Dost thou think, because thou art virtuous, there shall be no more cakes and ale?

WILLIAM SHAKESPEARE, TWELFTH NIGHT

AFTERNOON TEA AND CAKES or biscuits was established in the 1820s, when the tea plantations in Assam, India began to yield cheap and plentiful tea. By the time Victoria became queen, it was an indispensable and agreeable daily ritual. Victorian cooks began to expand their cake repertoire, helped by the introduction of raising agents such as baking powder and bicarbonate of soda in the mid-19th century. For the next century, at least, the tea-tables of the upper- and middle-class households were graced by such delicious confections as seed cake, plum cake, Savoy biscuits, macaroons, meringues, gingerbread, and sponges of all kinds.

A Teatime Selection

The recipes in this book can only show a selection of the many mouthwatering cakes and biscuits perfected by the Victorian cook. The recipes are based on authentic sources, adapted for modern tastes and for the smaller families of today.

MRS BEETON'S
CAKE-MAKING HINTS

1 **Break eggs separately into a cup before adding to a mixture, in case any are bad.**
2 **Wash and thoroughly dry all dried fruit.**
3 **Soften butter by warming it gently before creaming it.**
4 **Cover large cakes with a sheet of greaseproof paper during cooking to prevent burning.**
5 **To test a cake's progress in cooking, push a clean knife blade into its centre; if it emerges sticky, the cake is not done.**

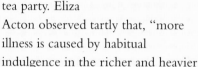

Not everyone approved of this perpetual tea party. Eliza Acton observed tartly that, "more illness is caused by habitual indulgence in the richer and heavier kinds of cakes than could easily be credited by persons who have given no attention to the matter". She was more kindly disposed to meringues, sponge cakes and biscuits, which she considered to be "the least objectionable". However, this did not prevent her from publishing some of the most delectable recipes for such "sweet poisons" as Fine Almond Cake and Pound Cake, adapted versions of which are to be found in this book.

CAKE TINS

It was very unusual for Victorian recipes – even those compiled by the meticulous Eliza Acton – to give the size of cake tin required. The experienced cook would know, simply by looking at the amount of cake batter, how large the tin should be. Unless otherwise stated, the large cakes in this book require a standard 8in/20cm round tin.

Cookies & Biscuits

WHAT THE ENGLISH TODAY CALL BISCUITS ARE MUCH BETTER DESCRIBED AS COOKIES. COOKIE IS DERIVED FROM THE DUTCH WORD FOR "LITTLE CAKE". IT HAS BEEN USED SINCE THE 18TH CENTURY IN SCOTLAND AND AMERICA, AND IS NOW FINDING ITS WAY BACK TO ENGLAND. THE WORD BISCUIT COMES FROM THE FRENCH *BIS-CUIT* AND ORIGINALLY REFERRED TO VERY DRY PRODUCTS SUCH AS RUSKS OR SEA BISCUITS.

ALL THE CAKES AND COOKIES YOU NEED
FOR A SUMPTUOUS VICTORIAN TEATIME SPREAD

MACAROONS

Macaroons are a light Continental confection much appreciated by the Victorians, who loved anything flavoured with almond. These are based on Mrs Beeton's recipe.

INGREDIENTS

3 Egg Whites
8oz/225g Ground Almonds
8oz/225g Caster Sugar
Rice Paper
Flaked Almonds

METHOD

❦ Place the egg whites in a very clean mixing bowl and whisk until they form stiff peaks. Gently fold in the ground almonds and the caster sugar until they are evenly incorporated.

❦ Spoon the mixture on to rice paper lined baking sheets using a teaspoon, leaving space between each macaroon to allow them to spread, and place a piece of flaked almond on top of each one.

❦ Bake at 160°C/325°F/gas mark 3 until they turn a light brown colour, then remove any excess rice paper and cool on wire racks.

COOK'S TIP

For lighter macaroons, add a little more egg white.

MACAROONS AND LITTLE RATAFIAS

Holy Macaroons

Macaroons were probably invented in Italy, but have been made in France for centuries. After the French Revolution, it became the custom for convent nuns to make them for sale.

Little Maccaroons, sweet as
sugar and almonds can make them
✦✦
SIR JAMES GRANT

RATAFIAS

Ratafias are essentially miniature macaroons. The egg white and sugar mixture is piped through an icing bag to make tiny biscuits. They get their name from ratafia wine, either because they were made to be eaten with it, or because they were almond flavoured. Ratafia was a fruit liqueur, usually based on cherries, peaches or almonds. It was drunk mid-morning, and considered a great tonic.

SCOTCH SHORTBREAD

This is a traditional shortbread and very delicious. It is based on Mrs Beeton's recipe.

INGREDIENTS

8oz/225g Butter
1lb/450g Plain Flour
2oz/50g Caster Sugar
½oz/12g Caraway Seeds
1oz/25g Chopped Almonds
Candied Peel for Decoration

METHOD

❧ Place the butter in a mixing bowl and cream with a wooden spoon until soft. Add the flour in several stages, beating thoroughly between each addition. Add the sugar, caraway seeds and almonds and mix to a smooth paste using your hands.

❧ Split the prepared shortbread into three equal pieces and roll each one into a rectangle about 1in/25mm thick. Prick well with a fork, decorate with a few pieces of candied peel and place on greased baking sheets.

❧ Cook at 180°C/350°F/gas mark 4 for 25 minutes.

A SELECTION OF SHORTBREAD

BALMORAL SHORTBREAD

Decorated by Royalty

AT BUCKINGHAM PALACE, THE PATTERN PRICKED ON THE SHORTBREAD WAS ALWAYS THE SAME: THREE ROWS OF THREE DOTS, IN A DOMINO PATTERN.

This recipe comes direct from the royal kitchens. Queen Victoria used to eat a little of this delicious shortbread every day.

INGREDIENTS

8oz/225g Softened Butter
4oz/125g Caster Sugar
12oz/350g Plain Flour

METHOD

❧ Place the softened butter and caster sugar in a bowl and cream together. Sieve in the flour and using the fingertips gently work it into the mixture until a dough is formed.

❧ Roll out the bread very thinly and cut into biscuits using cutters. Prick the surface of each one with a fork.

❧ Place the finished biscuits on a greased baking sheet and cook at 180°C/350°F/gas mark 4 for 15 minutes.

IMPERIALS

❦

These zesty little cakes are based on a recipe from Eliza
Acton. She opined that they were "not very rich", and
therefore suitable for children. Perhaps they were accompanied
by Imperial Water, a kind of lemonade made from water,
lemons and cream of tartar.

INGREDIENTS

1lb / 450g Flour
6oz / 175g Butter
8oz / 225g Caster Sugar
6oz / 175g Currants
2oz / 50g Chopped Candied Peel
Grated Rind of 1 Lemon
4 Eggs

❦

*Learn to think
Imperially.*
JOSEPH
CHAMBERLAIN

METHOD

❦ Using the fingertips, rub the flour and butter together in a
bowl. When the mixture resembles fine breadcrumbs, stir in the
caster sugar, currants, chopped peel and grated lemon rind.

❦ Beat the eggs well in a separate bowl and add them gradually
to the mixture until well incorporated. Very lightly grease and flour
a baking sheet and, using forks, make small piles of the mixture
remembering to leave enough space between each to allow them to
spread during baking.

❦ Cook at 150°C/300°F/gas mark 2 for 20 minutes until they are
an even, pale brown colour.

Dessert Biscuits

These are based on Mrs Beeton's recipe; they taste good as they are but can be flavoured in various ways according to taste.

INGREDIENTS

4oz / 125g Butter

6oz / 175g Flour

1oz / 25g Ground Ginger

4oz / 125g Caster Sugar

2 Egg Yolks, Beaten

MAKES 24 BISCUITS

METHOD

❧ Place the butter in a basin and beat it with a wooden spoon until soft. Sieve the flour and ground ginger together and add it gradually to the butter, beating each addition well before adding the next.

❧ Stir in the caster sugar and the well-beaten egg yolks and continue to beat for a few minutes. Cover a baking sheet with a piece of buttered greaseproof paper and spoon on small amounts of the mixture, leaving sufficient space for the biscuits to spread while cooking.

❧ Bake at 150°C/300°F/gas mark 2 for about 20 minutes. Do not let the biscuits colour too much.

Mrs Beeton suggests that you

FLAVOUR THESE BISCUITS BY ADDING LEMON ESSENCE, ALMOND ESSENCE, CINNAMON OR CURRANTS WITH THE CASTER SUGAR. YOU COULD SPLIT THE MIXTURE IN HALF AND FLAVOUR EACH HALF DIFFERENTLY.

LIGHT AND TANGY JUMBLES AND LEMON BISCUITS

JUMBLES

These crisp, lemony biscuits were an established favourite a century or two before the Victorian era. Earlier recipes referred to them as "jumballs". The recipe given here is based on Eliza Acton's.

Jumbles were made in ring or roll shapes. "There were hearts and rounds, and jumbles, which playful youth slip over the forefinger before spoiling their annular outline".

OLIVER WENDELL HOLMES, ELSIE VENNER

INGREDIENTS

1lb/450g Flour
1lb/450g Caster Sugar
4 Eggs
6oz/175g Butter
Grated Rind of 2 Lemons
Freshly Grated Nutmeg

METHOD

❧ Sieve the flour and caster sugar into a bowl. Break the eggs into a separate bowl and beat thoroughly then add them to the flour and sugar and mix well.

❧ Melt the butter gently over a low heat before adding to the mixture along with the lemon rind and the grated nutmeg. Mix all the ingredients together and drop spoonfuls of the mixture on to greased baking sheets.

❧ Bake at 150°C/300°F/gas mark 2 for 30 minutes until crisp but pale in colour.

LEMON BISCUITS

These are based on a recipe from Mrs Beeton. They are very refreshing for afternoon tea or served with homemade ice cream or syllabub.

INGREDIENTS

12oz/350g Flour
3oz/75g Butter
6oz/175g Caster Sugar
Grated Rind of 1 lemon
4 Eggs
2tsp/10ml Fresh Lemon Juice

METHOD

❧ Sieve the flour into a mixing bowl and add the butter cut into small pieces. Using the tips of the fingers, gently rub the butter into the flour before adding the caster sugar and grated lemon rind.

❧ In a separate bowl whisk the eggs and lemon juice, add to the main ingredients and beat thoroughly. Take dessert-spoonfuls of the mixture and drop on to a greased baking sheet leaving a gap between each to allow for spreading during cooking.

❧ Cook at 180°C/350°F/gas mark 4 for 20 minutes or until the biscuits are a delicate shade of brown.

He said that few people had the intellectual resources sufficient to forgo the pleasures of wine. They could not otherwise contrive how to fill the interval between dinner and supper.

JAMES BOSWELL,
THE LIFE OF DR JOHNSON

WINE CAKES

These delicious wine flavoured biscuits are based on a Victorian recipe but have an unmistakably rakish 18th-century tang. Try them as sweet snacks to go with wine or serve them for dessert with Whipped Syllabub and fresh fruit purée.

INGREDIENTS

4oz/125g Butter
3–4 tbsp/50ml Red Wine
8oz/225g Flour
8oz/225g Caster Sugar
2 Eggs
Caraway Seeds
Beaten Egg to Glaze

METHOD

❦ Soften the butter in a mixing bowl and add the wine a little at a time until well mixed. Mix the flour and caster sugar and sieve into the bowl in stages, stirring between each addition.

❦ Lightly beat the eggs and add to the mixture along with a few caraway seeds to form a firm paste that can be rolled out. Turn the paste out on to a very lightly floured surface and roll out thinly, using the top of a cup or tumbler cut the cakes from the paste and place on a baking sheet.

❦ Lightly brush the tops with a little beaten egg and sprinkle with caster sugar. Bake at 210°C/425°F/gas mark 7 for 10 minutes and allow to cool before serving.

THE ROYAL JUBILEES

When Albert, her beloved husband, died in 1861, the Queen retired from public life. In 1887, the prime minister Benjamin Disraeli persuaded her to publicly celebrate 50 years on the throne with the Golden Jubilee, followed a decade later by the Diamond Jubilee, "a great festival of empire".

The enthusiastic reception I met with on the occasion of my Jubilee has touched me most deeply.

QUEEN
VICTORIA

JUBILEE TEA CAKE

*F*ar more sophisticated than its name implies, this can be eaten at teatime but also make a most impressive dessert served with a little ice cream. This is based on an authentic Victorian recipe, perhaps invented to celebrate the two Royal Jubilees of 1887 and 1897.

INGREDIENTS

5tbsp/75ml Fresh Cream
3–4 tbsp/50ml Water
2oz/50g Butter
1oz/25g Caster Sugar
3oz/75g Ground Almonds
4 Eggs
Vanilla Essence
6oz/175g Icing Sugar
1–2 tbsp/25ml Water
Almond Flavouring
Fresh Fruit to Garnish

Hurrah! Hurrah! We bring the Jubilee!
H.G. WORK,
MARCHING THROUGH GEORGIA

METHOD

❦ Place the cream, 3 to 4 tbsps/50ml water, butter and caster sugar in a saucepan and bring to the boil. Once boiling, add the ground almonds and stir well to incorporate them into the liquid, reduce the heat to a simmer and allow the mixture to cook for a few minutes.

❦ Separate the eggs and beat the yolks with a few drops of vanilla essence, then take the almond mixture from the heat and slowly add it to the egg yolks, beating well all the time. Take two of the egg whites and whisk them until they form stiff peaks and carefully fold them into the prepared mixture.

❦ Grease a ring mould and line it with greaseproof paper, dust lightly with a little flour and pour in the cake mixture. Bake at 180°C/350°F/gas mark 4 for about 25 minutes until the cake has turned a pale brown colour. Remove the cake from the mould and place on a wire rack to cool.

❦ To make the icing, sieve the icing sugar into a bowl and add the water a little at a time until the icing is smooth and of the correct consistency. Add a few drops of almond flavouring and pour over the cake only when it has completely cooled. Garnish with fresh fruit such as sliced apple.

THREADNEEDLE STREET BISCUITS

This is recipe is based on one from Eliza Acton. It produces austere, dignified, semi-sweet biscuits, rather like digestives, that would have been very suitable for the sober junketings of bankers and shareholders.

INGREDIENTS

2lb/900g Flour

3oz/75g Butter

4oz/125g Caster Sugar

Caraway Seeds (Optional)

Milk

METHOD

❦ Sieve the flour into a large mixing bowl, add the butter and rub through using the fingertips until it resembles fine breadcrumbs. Sieve the sugar into the basin and add a few caraway seeds if desired. Stir together well.

❦ Adding a little milk at a time, stir the mixture with a wooden spoon until it forms a firm paste that is suitable for rolling out. Turn the paste out on to a lightly floured work surface and knead until it is very smooth, then roll it out until it is about ⅓in/8mm thick. Cut the biscuits out using small, square cutters and place them on baking sheets.

❦ Bake at 150°C/300°F/gas mark 2 until the biscuits are crisp all over. When cooked, remove them from the oven and cool on wire racks prior to serving.

THE BANK OF ENGLAND *is known as the Old Lady of Threadneedle Street, which is where it stands in the City of London.*

THREADNEEDLE STREET BISCUITS

Harris and I would go down in the morning…and George, who would not be able to get away from the City till the afternoon (George goes to sleep at a bank from ten to four each day, except Saturdays, when they wake him up and put him outside at two), would meet us there.

J. K. JEROME,
THREE MEN IN A BOAT

Caraway Seeds

Victorian cooks used caraway seeds liberally in cakes, sweets and biscuits. Perhaps the attraction was medicinal; caraway seeds are reputed to aid the digestion and combat flatulence.

MEREWORTH BISCUITS

These are light, crisp biscuits to eat buttered or with soft cheese. The recipe is based on one from Lady Sarah Lindsay's Choice Recipes (1883). Mereworth, where they were first made, is a stately home in Kent.

INGREDIENTS

8oz/225g Plain Flour
Pinch of Salt
1oz/25g Butter
Hot Milk

COOK'S TIP

This recipe produces a great number of biscuits so storing them in an air-tight tin until required is a good idea.

METHOD

❧ Add a pinch of salt to the flour and sieve it into a bowl. Rub the butter into the flour and slowly add sufficient hot milk to make a soft dough.

❧ Turn the dough out on to a lightly floured surface and knead well for a few minutes. Take small amounts of the dough, roll out very thinly and cut into rounds using a plain cutter.

❧ Place on baking sheets and cook at 210°C/425°F/gas mark 7 until they have browned and risen a little (about 5 minutes).

The Stately homes of England
How beautiful they stand
Amidst their tall ancestral trees
O'er all the pleasant land!

FELICIA HEMANS

FINE WHITE BREAD BISCUITS

These are based on a recipe from Eliza Acton called Aunt Charlotte's Biscuits; she describes them as "very simple and very good". Use them as you would cream crackers or Bath Olivers.

COOK'S TIP

If you are making white bread, use up surplus dough by making these biscuits, kneading 1oz/50g butter into each 1lb/450g of dough after it has risen.

INGREDIENTS

1oz/25g Fresh Yeast
1½pt/900ml Warm Water
3lb/1.5kg White Flour
2tsp/10ml Salt
½oz/12g Sugar
5oz/150g Butter

METHOD

Put the yeast in a bowl and stir in a little of the warm water. Put to one side for 10 minutes to froth. Sieve the flour and salt together into a mixing bowl, add the sugar and rub in 2oz/50g of the butter. Using your hand, stir in the frothing yeast mixture and the rest of the warm water to produce a soft dough. Knead for a few minutes on a floured board, cover and place in a warm cupboard for 1½ hours until it has doubled in size.

Once the dough has proven, turn it out on to the board and knock the air out by kneading it again. Break the remaining 3oz/75g of butter into small pieces and work them thoroughly into the dough.

Leave for another 30 minutes to rise again, then flatten the dough out until it is roughly ¼ in/6mm thick. Prick all over with a fork and cut out the biscuits using cutters. Place on baking sheets and cook at 180°C/350°F/gas mark 4 for about 10 minutes.

GINGER BREAD

This is based on Andrew's Gingerbread, one of Mrs Beeton's many gingerbread recipes. This is a quick, simple recipe, ideal for children to cook themselves.

INGREDIENTS

6oz/175g Butter
4oz/125g Caster Sugar
1/3pt/175ml Golden Syrup
2 Eggs
1oz/25g Ground Ginger
1lb 4oz/575g Plain Flour

METHOD

❦ Place the butter, sugar and golden syrup into a bowl and beat until well creamed together. Beat the eggs one at a time and add to the mixture ensuring they are well mixed in.

❦ Sift together the ginger and flour and slowly add to the bowl, stirring all the time, until the bread is very thick.

❦ Roll out the gingerbread thinly on a lightly floured board and cut into biscuits using cutters. Bake at 180°C/350°F/gas mark 4 for about 20 to 25 minutes until the biscuits have hardened and are darker in colour.

THE GILT ON THE GINGERBREAD

Gingerbread has a long history. In medieval times, it was made with honey, cooked in dark brown slabs and studded with gilded leaves and cloves to look like the tooled leather worn by noble knights.

Our boyish days look very merry to us now, all nutting, hoop, and gingerbread.

J.K. JEROME
IDLE THOUGHTS OF AN
IDLE FELLOW

RICH GINGERBREAD NUTS

These are very dressy ginger nuts, based on Mrs Beeton's recipe. They are delicious for a special occasion tea, or as a gift for gingerbread fans.

INGREDIENTS

4oz/125g Butter
1lb/450g Treacle
1lb/450g Coarse Brown Sugar
2oz/50g Ground Ginger
2oz/50g Chopped Candied Peel
1oz/25g Ground Caraway Seeds
1 Egg
Flour

METHOD

❦ Place the butter in a small pan and warm over a low heat until it has just melted. Pass the melted butter through a clean piece of muslin to remove any impurities. Pour this clarified butter into a basin containing the treacle and add to it the brown sugar and the ground ginger.

❦ Mix together well, stirring in the chopped peel and ground caraway seeds as you mix. Add the beaten egg and sufficient flour, a little at a time, until a good stiff paste is formed.

❦ Sprinkle some flour over a board and roll out the gingerbread evenly, then cut into any shapes you desire and place on greased baking sheets. Bake at 160°C/325°F/gas mark 3 for 30 minutes.

THICK GINGERBREAD

This recipe, based on Mrs Beeton's, produces rich, thick slabs of spicy gingerbread. Children love it; it's very good for bonfire parties or Hallowe'en.

INGREDIENTS

1lb 8oz / 700g Flour
4oz / 125g Soft Brown Sugar
1oz / 25g Ground Ginger
½oz / 12g Ground Allspice
4oz / 125g Butter
1lb / 450g Treacle
½oz / 12g Bicarbonate of Soda
¼pt / 150ml Warm Milk
3 Eggs
1 Egg Yolk for Glazing

METHOD

❦ Sieve the flour into a large basin and mix in the brown sugar, ginger and allspice. Melt the butter and treacle over a low heat and stir into the other ingredients along with the bicarbonate of soda dissolved in the warm milk.

❦ Lightly whisk the eggs and beat into the gingerbread until a smooth dough is formed.

❦ Pour the mixture into a greased tin and cook at 180°C/350°F/gas mark 4 for approximately one hour. A few minutes before the cooking is complete, brush the top with beaten egg and return it to the oven.

THICK GINGERBREAD TO SWEETEN LAZY SUNDAY AFTERNOONS.

SAVOY CAKE

This is based on Mrs Beeton's recipe. According to her, it is "a very nice cake for dessert, and may be iced for a supper table, or cut into slices and spread with jam".

INGREDIENTS

6 Eggs
8oz/225g Caster Sugar
Grated Rind of 1 Lemon
Almond Essence
12oz/350g Flour

METHOD

❧ Separate the eggs and beat the yolks with the caster sugar, lemon rind and a few drops of almond essence.

❧ In a clean bowl, whisk the egg whites until they form peaks and fold them into the yolks. Beat together well with a whisk for a few minutes then sieve in the flour and fold into the yolk and sugar mixture.

❧ Pour the mixture into a greased and floured loose-bottomed tin and bake at 180°C/350°F/gas mark 4 for 1½ hours or until a skewer inserted into the cake comes out cleanly.

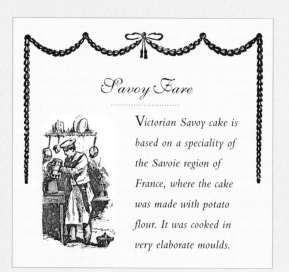

Savoy Fare

Victorian Savoy cake is based on a speciality of the Savoie region of France, where the cake was made with potato flour. It was cooked in very elaborate moulds.

The dessert was now put upon the table. In the middle there was a Savoy cake, in the shape of a temple with a melon-sectioned dome; ... then, on the left a cream cheese swam in a shallow bowl, and in another bowl on the right a pile of huge strawberries lightly crushed were running with juice.

EMILE ZOLA, L'ASSOMMOIR

SAVOY BISCUITS

Savoy Biscuits are delectable on their own but also form an intrinsic part of complicated dishes such as Charlotte Russe and Cabinet Pudding. This recipe is based on Mrs Beeton's.

INGREDIENTS

4 Eggs
6oz/175g Caster Sugar
Grated Rind of 1 Lemon
6oz/175g Plain Flour

METHOD

❧ Separate the eggs, place the yolks in a mixing bowl and beat well. Add the caster sugar and lemon rind and continue beating for a good 10 minutes. Slowly add the flour to the bowl a little at a time and beat thoroughly between each addition.

❧ In a clean bowl whisk the egg whites until they form stiff peaks and fold them into the biscuit mixture before beating all the ingredients together briefly.

❧ Take a spoonful at a time of the mixture and allow it to run on to greased baking sheets to form finger shapes. Bake at 180°C/350°F/gas mark 4 until lightly browned, but do keep a watchful eye as they cook quickly and can burn soon after.

LIGHT AND GOLDEN SAVOY CAKES AND SAVOY BISCUITS

MADEIRA CAKE

This cake was made to be eaten with Madeira wine when visitors called in the late morning. It is just as enjoyable at the tea-table. This recipe is based on Eliza Acton's A Good Madeira Cake.

COOK'S TIP

A light dusting of icing sugar prior to serving finishes this delicious, tangy cake very nicely.

INGREDIENTS

4oz / 125g Butter
6oz / 175g Caster Sugar
4 Eggs
Grated Rind of 1 Lemon
6oz / 175g Flour
Pinch of Salt

METHOD

❧ Put the butter and caster sugar in a bowl and cream together until light in colour. Beat in the eggs one at a time and add the grated lemon rind.

❧ Sieve the flour and salt into the basin and gently fold into the cake mixture using a wooden spoon.

❧ Pour the prepared cake mixture into a well greased, loose-bottomed cake tin and bake at 180°C/350°F/gas mark 4 for 1½ hours until nicely browned on top.

MADEIRA WINE

MADEIRA is one of the finest of the fortified dessert wines. It comes from Madeira, made from grapes grown on vines imported to the island from Cyprus in the 15th century. It is very sweet to today's taste, but was a great favourite with the Victorians.

MADEIRA CAKE TO PARTNER MADEIRA WINE

Sponge Cake

This is an old-fashioned sponge cake, feathery light
as it contains no fat. The cake is suitable for cooking in fanciful
moulds or as a basis for such sweet delights as Hedgehog Pudding.
This is based on Mrs Beeton's recipe.

INGREDIENTS

4 Eggs
8oz/225g Caster Sugar
Grated Rind of 1 Lemon
6oz/175g Flour

COOK'S TIP

The air incorporated into the
egg whites is a major factor in this
cake's lightness, so do be gentle
during the preparation.

METHOD

❦ Separate the eggs and lightly beat the yolks. Place them in a
saucepan with the caster sugar and place over a gentle heat, stir until
the sugar has dissolved but do not allow the pan to get too hot.

❦ Take the mixture from the heat and pour it into a bowl, add the
grated lemon rind and mix well. Sieve in the flour in several stages,
stirring well between each addition and fold in the egg whites which
have been whisked to stiff peak stage.

❦ Beat the cake mixture well for a few minutes then pour it into a loose-
bottomed cake tin that has been greased and sprinkled with caster sugar.
Bake the cake immediately at 180°C/350°F/gas mark 4 for 1 1/2 hours.

TRADITIONAL SPONGE CAKE
AND VICTORIA SANDWICH

HEDGEHOG PUDDING
This is made by cooking a sponge cake in an oval
shape, then soaking it in sherry to saturation point. Flaked
almonds, closely packed in rows all over the cake, form the
hedgehog "prickles". Serve it in a moat of rich custard.

VICTORIA SANDWICH

This variation on the sponge, named
for the Queen, is based on Mrs Beeton's recipe.

INGREDIENTS

8oz/225g Butter	Grated Rind of 1 Lemon
8oz/225g Caster Sugar	Your Favourite Jam for Filling
4 Eggs	Icing Sugar
8oz/225g Flour	
Pinch of Salt	

METHOD

❦ Place the butter and sugar in a bowl and beat with a wooden spoon
until pale and soft. Beat in the eggs one at a time until well incorporated.

❦ Fold in the sieved flour and salt and add the grated lemon rind.
Stir for a few minutes then pour the cake mixture into a greased
sponge tin and bake for 20 minutes at 180°C/350°F/gas mark 4.

❦ When the sponge is firm to the touch remove it from the oven and
cool on a wire rack. Split the cake through the middle and fill with jam,
cut into fingers and serve immediately, dusted with a little icing sugar.

It was the Victorian cooks WHO INTRODUCED THE
IDEA OF ADDING BUTTER TO THE TRADITIONAL
ENGLISH SPONGE MIXTURE; THIS PRODUCED A
MORE SOLID MIX THAT BAKED RATHER FLATTER.
THE RESULTING CAKES COULD BE SANDWICHED
TOGETHER TO CONSTRUCT THE KIND OF "BUILT
CAKE" SO SATISFYING TO THE ENGINEERING
MENTALITY OF MANY VICTORIANS.

ITALIAN MERINGUES

These are based on Eliza Acton's recipe. They are intended to be fastened together with whipped cream.

COOK'S TIP

Use a kitchen fork to flick melted chocolate over the finished meringues to produce very attractive results.

INGREDIENTS

1lb / 450g Caster Sugar
1pt / 600ml Fresh Water
4 Egg Whites

METHOD

❦ Place the sugar and water in a saucepan and boil until the solution starts to turn white in the pan. Turn off the heat and allow it to stand for 2 to 3 minutes, stirring continuously to keep the sugar soft.

❦ Beat the egg whites until they form stiff peaks then quickly combine the sugar and egg whites to form a meringue that can hold its shape when moulded.

❦ Take teaspoon-sized amounts of the meringue and place on baking sheets. Cook in a very slow oven, 130°C/250°F/gas mark ½ until they have hardened but show no signs of colouring.

Sweet King

THE FIRST MERINGUES made in France were offered to Duke Stanislaus of Lorraine, the deposed King of Poland and father in law of Louis XV. Stanislaus was a connoisseur of sweet things; he is credited with the invention of the Rum Baba.

MERINGUES

These are rather lighter than the sugar syrup based Italian meringues; they are based on Mrs Beeton's recipe. You can pile them altogether to make a glorious dessert.

INGREDIENTS

4 Egg Whites
8oz / 225g Caster Sugar
Fresh Double Cream
Fresh Soft Fruit to Decorate (Optional)

He insisted on her partaking of a large glass of lemonade and three meringues.

MRS CATTYN,
THE QUAKER GRANDMOTHER

THE ROYAL CONNECTION

Meringues are said to have been invented in 1720 by a Swiss pastry cook named Gasparini. At the time, he was working in Mehrinyghen, a town in Saxe-Coburg-Gotha, the birthplace of both Queen Victoria's beloved consort Albert, and her mother, Victoria Louise.

Let them eat Meringue

MARIE-ANTOINETTE, THE DOOMED QUEEN OF FRANCE, MADE HER OWN MERINGUES IN HER PLAY-KITCHEN AT LE PETIT TRIANON PALACE AT VERSAILLES.

COOK'S TIP

When whisking, it is most important that the mixture is treated carefully as the more air incorporated into the mixture the lighter the finished meringues will be.

METHOD

❦ Place the egg whites in a clean bowl and whisk until they form stiff peaks. Using a metal spoon, take one tablespoonful of the caster sugar and stir lightly into the egg whites. Continue whisking the meringue and slowly add the remaining sugar.

❦ Cover a baking tray with greaseproof paper and lightly oil the surface. Take tablespoons of the meringue and place them a small distance apart and roughly the same size on the paper. Bake in a very cool oven, 130°C/250°F/ gas mark ½, for 2 hours until they begin to colour.

❦ Remove them from the oven and allow to cool before sandwiching them together with some fresh whipped cream and decorating with fresh raspberries or slices of fresh strawberry.

LIGHT AND LUSCIOUS MERINGUES

SEED CAKE

*S*eed Cake or Seedy Cake is a traditional country cake, often eaten at harvest time, but popular all the year round. This is based on Mrs Beeton's recipe for A Very Good Seed Cake and makes a deliciously moist cake.

INGREDIENTS

1lb / 450g Butter
1lb / 450g Flour
12oz / 350g Caster Sugar
1oz / 25g Caraway Seeds
Grated Nutmeg
6 Eggs
3–4 tbsp / 50ml Brandy

COOK'S TIP

This cake would be equally good made with currants instead of caraway seeds, according to Mrs Beeton.

METHOD

❦ Place the butter in a mixing bowl and beat until soft using a wooden spoon. Sieve in the flour and add the caster sugar, caraway seeds and a little grated nutmeg and mix thoroughly.

❦ Break the eggs into a separate bowl, beat lightly and add to the cake mixture along with the brandy. Beat all the ingredients together for a few minutes then pour into a lightly-greased, loose-based cake tin.

❦ Cook at 180°C/350°F/gas mark 4 for 1½ hours.

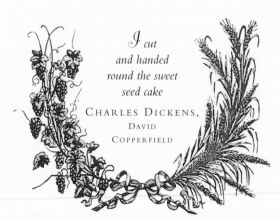

I cut and handed round the sweet seed cake

CHARLES DICKENS,
DAVID COPPERFIELD

WHOLESOME SEED CAKE, IDEAL FOR EVERYDAY TEATIMES

SPICY SYRUP AND RAISIN CAKE

This is based on a Mrs Beeton recipe called Aunt Betsey's Cake. You can just imagine an indulgent auntie making this delicious, sticky, fruit cake for her favourite nieces and nephews.

INGREDIENTS

2oz/50g Butter

8oz/225g Caster Sugar

2 Eggs

1tsp/5g Bicarbonate of Soda

⅕pt/125ml Cold Water

1lb 4oz/575g Flour

4oz/125g Golden Syrup

8oz/225g Raisins

Pinch each of Cinnamon, Ground Cloves
and Ground Mace

COOK'S TIP

You can use this mixture to make small cakes in patty pans if a large one is impracticable

METHOD

❦ Place the butter and caster sugar in a mixing bowl and cream together until light in colour. Add the eggs one at a time and beat into the mixture until well incorporated.

❦ Dissolve the bicarbonate of soda in the cold water and add along with the remaining ingredients. Beat together thoroughly for a few minutes.

❦ Turn the cake mixture into a well greased square cake tin and bake at 180°C/350°F/gas mark 4 for 1½ hours.

GOLDEN SYRUP WAS FIRST MADE IN THE 1880S. IT IS PRODUCED AS A BY-PRODUCT DURING THE REFINING PROCESS OF CRYSTALLIZED SUGAR.

COCONUT CAKE

An elaborate coconut extravaganza, this cake is based on a recipe from Mrs Beeton.

INGREDIENTS

6oz/175g Butter
8oz/225g Caster Sugar
2 Eggs
1lb/450g Flour
½oz/12g Baking Powder
4oz/125g Desiccated Coconut
Grated Rind of 1 Lemon
Milk
Chocolate Icing for Decoration (see page 33)
Jam
Desiccated Coconut for Decoration

METHOD

❧ Place the butter and sugar together in a bowl and cream until pale in colour. Beat in the eggs one at a time and sieve in the flour and baking powder. Add the desiccated coconut and grated lemon rind and mix together well.

❧ Slowly add enough milk to bring the cake mixture to a batter-like consistency and divide it equally between two buttered sandwich tins. Bake at 180°C/350°F/gas mark 4 for about 25 minutes until well risen and golden, then remove the cakes from the oven and cool on wire racks.

❧ Sandwich the two halves together with a thick layer of jam and prepare a chocolate icing to coat the top of the cake. Melt a little more jam, brush over the sides of the cake and sprinkle with handfuls of coconut to decorate.

COCONUT ROCKS

These light, delicious coconut fancies are a favourite at children's tea parties. The recipe is based on one from Mrs Beeton.

INGREDIENTS

4oz/125g Butter
4oz/125g Caster Sugar
5oz/150g Flour
3oz/75g Desiccated Coconut
2 Eggs

METHOD

❧ Cream the butter and sugar together until light and fluffy. Slowly sieve in the flour and add the desiccated coconut, beating between each addition.

❧ Break the eggs into a bowl and lightly whisk before thoroughly beating into the cake mixture.

❧ Using a spoon, drop small amounts of the mixture on to greased baking sheets and bake at 210°C/425°F/gas mark 7 for 10 minutes.

COCONUTS

Coconuts were imported from the Caribbean and were extremely popular in the 19th century. Victorian cooks used them for cakes, biscuits, sweets and puddings; desiccated coconut was a very popular garnish.

DELICIOUS AND AROMATIC COFFEE CAKES

COFFEE CAKES

Delicious with morning coffee or hot chocolate, these
delicate little cakes are based on a genuine, but unattributed, Victorian recipe.

INGREDIENTS

4 Eggs

6oz/175g Caster Sugar

½oz/12g Strong Coffee Granules

1tsp/5g Baking Powder

4oz/125g Flour

Coffee, which makes the politician wise
And see through all things with
his half-shut eyes.

ALEXANDER POPE,
THE RAPE OF THE LOCK

Coffee in an Instant

The original Victorian recipe used
made-up coffee. Instant coffee was invented
by G. W. Washington, an Englishman
living in Guatemala, who noticed that when
steaming coffee cooled on the coffee pot
spout, it produced a fine powder. He
worked on a method to reproduce this
commercially and, in 1909,
instant coffee was created.

METHOD

❧ Break the four eggs into a bowl and add to them the caster sugar and coffee. Place the bowl over a saucepan of boiling water and whisk the contents until they have warmed. Remove the bowl and continue whisking until the mixture has cooled and become thick.

❧ Mix the baking powder into the flour and allow to warm a little in a very low oven. Gradually add it to the coffee mixture in several stages, mixing well between each addition. Pour the prepared cake mixture into cake tins that have been lightly buttered and floured and bake at 180°C/350°F/gas mark 4 for about 15 minutes.

❧ Remove them from the oven and turn out on to racks to cool. Dust with a little icing sugar or coat with a coffee icing and serve.

Fine Almond Cake

This cake is based on a recipe from Eliza Acton.
It is gorgeously rich but very refined; a little
goes a very long way.

INGREDIENTS

9oz/250g Fresh Almonds
12 Eggs
1lb/450g Caster Sugar
12oz/350g Flour
1lb/450g Butter
Grated Rind of 2 Lemons

METHOD

❦ Blanch the almonds to remove their skins, then
grind them to a paste in a pestle and mortar and put
them in a large mixing bowl. Break the dozen eggs
into a separate bowl and whisk until very light and
fluffy, then gradually mix them into the ground almonds.

❦ Mix together the sugar and flour and add to the
basin in several stages, stopping to beat the mixture
between each addition. Gently melt the butter in a
saucepan and pour it through a piece of clean muslin
to remove any sediment. Add this clarified butter to
the cake mixture in stages, beating very
thoroughly to incorporate before
adding any more.

❦ When all the butter has been
added, mix in the grated lemon rind and pour
the mixture into a large well-buttered cake tin. Bake
at 200°C/400°F/gas mark 6 for two hours.

Almond Overload

True almondaholics might like to follow Eliza Acton's suggestion and add an extra 3oz/75g blanched almonds to the mixture, in which case additional sugar (2oz/50g) and an extra egg will be needed.

COOK'S TIP

If the cake colours quickly, cover it with a piece of greaseproof paper to prevent it browning any more.

FINE ALMOND CAKE, VERY RICH AND VERY REFINED

PLAIN POUND CAKE

POUND CAKE, THE CENTREPIECE OF
THE FARMHOUSE TEA-TABLE

*P*ound cake means any kind of cake made with equal proportions
of flour, sugar and butter or fat. This version is based on Eliza
Acton's recipe. You can add various ingredients
to make your own family version.

INGREDIENTS

8oz/225g Butter
8oz/225g Caster Sugar
5 Eggs
8oz/225g Flour

METHOD

❦ Beat the butter to a cream in a mixing bowl, add the sugar and
continue beating until well mixed in. Separate the eggs and beat the
yolks into the butter in several stages.

❦ In a separate bowl beat the egg whites until they are stiff, then
spoon them into the mixing bowl and gently mix them into the cake.
Sieve the flour into the mixing bowl a little at a time and stir into the
cake mixture.

❦ Pour the mixture into a buttered cake tin and cook at 180°C/350°F/
gas mark 4 for 1 hour until well risen and nicely browned.

Queen Cakes

THESE ARE SMALL CAKES, USUALLY
HEART SHAPED, MADE FROM THE
MIXTURE INDICATED FOR POUND
CURRANT CAKE. SERVED WITH
CIDER, THEY WERE A SPECIALITY OF
VARIOUS LONDON INNS IN THE
18TH CENTURY.

COOK'S TIP

Eliza Acton turns
this into Pound
Currant Cake by
adding 8oz/25g currants
and some candied peel
before the flour is added.
The recipe can also be
turned into Irish
Speckled Bread with
the simple addition of
caraway seeds.

*H*e begged to recommend the pound cake from
his own personal experience.

FRANCES TROLLOPE,
CHARMING FELLOWS

It will have a great odour of
bohea and pound cake

WILLIAM THACKERAY,
MEN & COATS

CHOCOLATE SURPRISE

This lovely light cake is based on a recipe from Lady Shaftesbury, who calls it Surprise au Chocolat. The surprise happens when you cut the dark, chocolatey outside to reveal a pale, creamy inside.

INGREDIENTS

6 Eggs

8oz/225g Caster Sugar

2oz/50g Plain Flour

2oz/50g Cornflour

½pt/300ml Double Cream, Whipped

4oz/125g Bitter Chocolate

1oz/25g Unsalted Butter

4oz/125g Icing Sugar

3–4 tbsp/50ml Water

Chocolate for Grating

METHOD

❦ Separate the eggs and beat the yolks to a smooth paste with the caster sugar. Sieve the flour and cornflour into the bowl and fold into the mixture.

❦ In a sterilized bowl, whisk the egg whites until they form stiff peaks and fold them into the cake mixture. Line a 9in/23cm loose-bottomed cake tin with greaseproof paper and gently pour in the cake mixture. Bake at 180°C/350°F/gas mark 4 for 45 minutes.

❦ Allow the cooked sponge to cool for a few minutes, then carefully remove it from the tin and stand it on a wire rack to cool completely. Once cold, cut the cake in half, remove some of the crumbs from inside the two halves and fill the holes with the stiffly whipped double cream.

❦ Sandwich the cake back together again and cover completely with the icing. Decorate the finished cake with a little grated chocolate and chill before serving.

CHOCOLATE ICING

Break up the chocolate and place it in a bowl over a saucepan of simmering water to melt. Add the butter cut into small pieces and stir in the icing sugar; continue stirring until the mixture is smooth. Remove from the heat and add the water, allow the icing a little time to cool.

COOK'S TIP

It is essential that egg whites are folded into the mixture with the utmost care as the more air incorporated into the cake, the lighter it will be.

Eating Chocolate

Surprise au Chocolat would have been a very modern, sophisticated cake. Sweet chocolate for eating was not made until 1847, when it was invented by Fry & Sons in England. Milk chocolate was developed in Switzerland in 1876. In the 17th and 18th centuries, chocolate was bitter, and only used for drinking.

CHOCOLATE SURPRISE
TO DELIGHT DINNER GUESTS

SODA CAKE

❧

A wholesome cake, based on a recipe from Eliza Acton, who disapproved of rich cakes. It is economical and easy to make, ideal for daily teatime consumption.

COOK'S TIP

You can split the mixture in half to make two smaller cakes; in this case, the cooking time should be 45 minutes.

INGREDIENTS

1lb/450g Flour
6oz/175g Butter
8oz/225g Caster Sugar
¼pt/150ml Milk
3 Eggs, Beaten
Grated Rind of 1 Lemon
8oz/225g Currants
Good Pinch of Bicarbonate of Soda

❧❧❧

METHOD

❧ Sieve the flour into a mixing bowl and rub through the butter using the tips of the fingers until the mixture resembles fine breadcrumbs. Sieve in the caster sugar and stir until well incorporated.

❧ Bring the milk to the boil and pour into the bowl along with the beaten eggs, lemon rind and currants. Beat all the ingredients together for a few minutes, then add the bicarbonate of soda dissolved in a little milk and beat again for a couple of minutes longer.

❧ Pour the mixture into a well-greased mould and cook at 180°C/350°F/gas mark 4 for 1¼ hours. Insert a skewer into the centre of the cake; if it comes out cleanly, then the cake is ready.

If carefully made, it resembles a pound cake, but is much less expensive and far more wholesome, while it has the advantage of being very expeditiously prepared.

ELIZA ACTON
ON SODA CAKE

BAKING SODA

Eliza Acton warns against "too large a proportion, or a course quality of soda", as either will make the cake disagreeable. Bicarbonate of Soda, which produces carbon dioxide when mixed with liquid, was introduced as a raising agent in cooking in the mid-19th century.

Lawn Tennis

LAWN TENNIS is a 19th-century adaptation of the ancient royal game of tennis. It was developed in 1873 by Major Walter Wingfield, who called it "Sphairistike". The All England Croquet Club of Wimbledon took it up with enthusiasm, even adding the name Lawn Tennis to their title; the club sponsored the first World Lawn Tennis Championship in 1877.

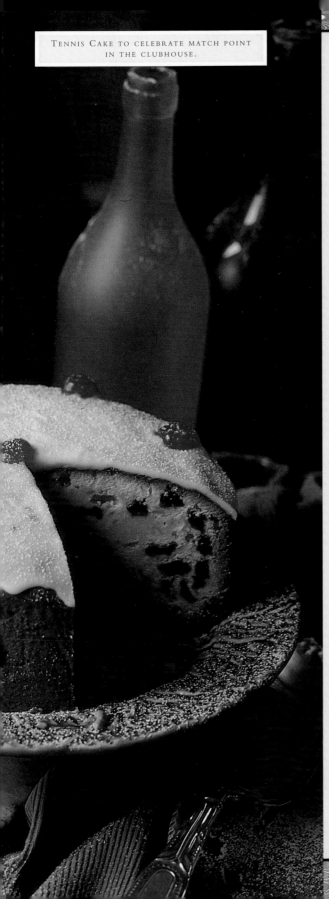

TENNIS CAKE

*Lawn tennis mania swept late Victorian England, and all over
suburbia, tennis clubs sprang up. Substantial teas were required in
the pavilion after strenuous sets; cucumber sandwiches and a rich
cake like this one, adapted from Mrs Beeton's recipe.*

INGREDIENTS

*8oz/225g Caster Sugar
12oz/350g Butter
Grated Rind and Juice of 1 Lemon
5 Eggs
1lb/450g Flour
8oz/225g Raisins
2oz/50g Chopped Blanched Almonds
3oz/75g Chopped Candied Peel
¼pt/150ml Milk
Icing for Decoration
Glacé Cherries*

METHOD

❦ Put the sugar and butter into a clean basin and cream together
until the mixture is light in colour. Beat in the lemon juice and grated
rind and add the eggs individually, beating each one into the mixture
thoroughly before adding the next.

❦ When all the eggs have been incorporated, sieve in the flour and add
the raisins, almonds and candied peel and mix well. If the mixture is a
little stiff, use some of the milk to bring it to a more cake-batter consistency.

❦ Line a loose-bottomed cake tin with greaseproof paper and brush
with melted butter, pour in the cake mixture and bake at 180°C/
350°F/gas mark 4 for 1½ hours. Turn the finished cake out on to a
wire rack to cool before decorating with white icing and glacé cherries.

*And now came the brief bright
season of rustic entertainments…lawn
tennis – archery – water parties.*

MARY ELIZABETH BRADDON,
MT ROYAL

PLUM CAKE

Plum Cake was a staple at the Victorian tea-table; there are as many recipes as there are cooks, but this one is based on Mrs Beeton's Nice Plum Cake.

INGREDIENTS

1lb/450g Flour
8oz/225g Caster Sugar
8oz/225g Currants
2oz/50g Chopped Candied Peel
4oz/125g Butter
½pt/300ml Milk
1tsp/5ml Bicarbonate of Soda
1–2 tbsp/25ml Milk

METHOD

❧ Sieve the flour into a mixing bowl and add the caster sugar, currants and candied peel. In a separate bowl beat the butter until soft. Add to the other ingredients and bind the whole together with the ½pt/300ml of milk.

❧ Make a paste using the bicarbonate of soda and remaining milk, add to the cake mixture and beat thoroughly for a few minutes until all of the ingredients are well combined.

❧ Turn the dough into a well buttered tin and bake at 180°C/350°F/gas mark 4 for 1½ hours.

THE LION AND THE UNICORN

The Lion and the Unicorn were fighting for the crown;
The Lion beat the Unicorn all round the town.
Some gave them white bread, some gave them brown;
Some gave them plum-cake and drummed them out of town.

NURSERY RHYME

PLUM CAKE, THE TRADITIONAL FAVOURITE

39

CHRISTMAS CAKE, THE CENTREPIECE
OF THE FESTIVE TEA-TABLE

CHRISTMAS CAKE

The Victorian family Christmas would not have been complete without a glorious, rich and enormous Christmas cake. This is based on Mrs Beeton's Christmas Cake No.1. She advises that it can be baked "in one or more cakes as desired", as it makes such a huge quantity. You can make the cakes six weeks before Christmas as long as you keep them wrapped in foil and stored in tins.

COOK'S TIP

Cover the cake with a sheet of greaseproof paper during the second half of its cooking time to prevent the top from burning.

INGREDIENTS

8oz / 225g Butter
8oz / 225g Caster Sugar
4 Eggs
1lb / 450g Flour
1/4oz / 6g Baking Powder
8oz / 225g Sultanas
8oz / 225g Currants
6oz / 175g Chopped Mixed Peel
Milk

METHOD

In a large mixing bowl cream together the butter and sugar until pale in colour. Add the eggs individually, making sure each is thoroughly beaten into the butter before adding the next.

Mix together the flour and baking powder and pass them through a sieve a couple of times to ensure the baking powder is evenly distributed through the flour. Add to the cake and mix well, then add the fruit and chopped peel and beat thoroughly. Carefully add sufficient milk to the mixture to moisten it to a good cake-batter consistency.

Line a good-sized cake tin with greaseproof paper and grease it thoroughly. You may prefer to use two or more cake tins, as this recipe makes almost 4lb/1.8kg of cake. Pour in the cake mixture and smooth over the surface. Bake at 150°C/300°F/gas mark 2 for 3 to 4 hours.

INDEX

A

Acton, Eliza, cake eating 6
almonds
  coffee cakes 30
  fine almond cake 31
  macaroons 8

B

baking powder 6
Bank of England 15
bicarbonate of soda 6, 34, 34
biscuits
  coconut rocks 28
  derivation 6
  dessert 11
  fine white bread 17
  jumbles 12
  lemon 12
  Mereworth 16
  Savoy 20
  Threadneedle Street 15
  wine cakes 13
bread
  fine white biscuits 17
  Irish speckled 32
butter, sponge cakes 23, 33

C

cakes
  chocolate surprise 33
  Christmas 40
  coconut 28
  coffee 29
  fine almond 31
  Imperials 10
  Madeira 22
  making 6
  plum 38
  pound 32
  Queen 32
  Savoy 20
  seed 26
  soda 34
  spicy syrup and raisin 27
  sponge 23
  tennis 37
  Victoria sandwich 23
caraway seeds 15, 26
chocolate 33
Choice Recipes (Lindsay) 16
coconuts 28
coffee 29
cookies, derivation 6

E

eggs 6

G

Gasparini 24
gingerbread 18, 19
  rich nuts 18
golden syrup

I

icing, chocolate 33

J

Jubilees, Royal 14
jumbles 12

L

lawn tennis 35, 37
lemonade, Imperial Water 10
Lindsay, Lady Sarah, *Choice Recipes* 16
liqueurs, ratafia 8

M

macaroons 8
Madeira wine 22
Marie-Antoinette, Queen 24
meringues 24

P

puddings, Hedgehog 23

R

raisins, syrup and raisin cake 27
ratafias 8

S

Shaftesbury, Lady, *Surprise au Chocolat* 33
shortbread 9
Stanislaus, Duke of Lorraine 24

T

tea, afternoon 6
tea cakes, Jubilee 14

V

Victoria, Queen 9, 14

W

wine, cakes 13
Wingfield, Major Walter 36